Originally published in 1989.
This edition updated and published in 2007 by
Ravette Publishing.

Printed and bound in Malta
for Ravette Publishing Limited,
Unit 3, Tristar Centre,
Star Road, Partridge Green,
West Sussex RH13 8RA

ISBN: 978-1-84161-290-4

Contents

PART 1: THE STORY OF THE FILM

The summer of 1963. The Houseman family –
Dr. Houseman, his wife Marge and their two
daughters, Lisa and Baby – are going on holiday.
Baby doesn't think that she'll ever meet a guy as
great as her Dad. She puts her arms round his
neck as he drives the car up the mountain road.

The family's holiday destination, Kellerman's Mountain House, comes into view. The car moves up the drive. Holidaymakers can be seen enjoying themselves in the sunshine.

Some forthcoming amusements are being announced through a loud-hailer as the family climb out of their car. The Housemans are welcomed by Max Kellerman, the owner of the holiday camp. We learn that Dr. Houseman once saved Max Kellerman's life.

In the open-air ballroom beside the lake, a Merengue dancing class has just begun. Penny, the dancing teacher, flashes her skirts as she encourages the holidaymakers to join in.

Penny organises a dancing-game with gentlemen on the outside and ladies on the inside. When it is time to pick a partner, Penny chooses Dr. Houseman and Baby finds herself dancing with old Mrs Schumaker.

In the evening, Baby leaves the family chalet to take a look around the camp. It is quiet and the lights glimmer mysteriously. Baby mounts the steps of the main building and listens in on a conversation between Max Kellerman and his employees. He is advising them how to behave towards their guests, especially the women.

Johnny Castle, the leader of the entertainment staff, appears with his team of dancers. Baby is attracted to him immediately.

Baby listens to the warning Johnny is given. The waiters, who are university students from Harvard and Yale, are allowed to flirt with the guests. Johnny and the entertainment staff are forbidden even to speak to them unless they're giving lessons.

At the supper table, Max Kellerman introduces his grandson, Neil. Neil Kellerman is attending a Hotel Management College. He is conceited and imagines Baby will be attracted to him.

The ballroom. The band plays some lively, swing music and Tito, the band-leader, performs a tap-dance on stage before being joined by Max Kellerman for a little duet.

Penny and Johnny appear. The two dancing instructors are supposed to dance with the guests, but instead they dance the Mambo together. Their performance clears the dancefloor and brings applause from the guests, but Kellerman disapproves. He tells them to stop.

Later that evening, Neil Kellerman persuades Baby to take part in the variety show. She is sawn in half by a magician and, by way of a prize, is presented with a live chicken with a bow round its neck. Thankfully, Baby escapes from the stage.

Baby goes out for some fresh air and meets Billy, Johnny's cousin. She helps Billy to carry some water-melons to the staff quarters. Billy takes Baby into the staff dancefloor where she encounters Dirty Dancing for the first time.

Penny and Johnny enter and are greeted enthusiastically by their fellow dancers. Watching them, Billy explains to Baby that they are not lovers, despite the closeness of their dancing.

Johnny spots Baby and invites her to join in the dancing.

Baby experiences Dirty Dancing for the first time. She is embarrassed by the erotic movements of the dance, yet fascinated by them at the same time. Anxiously, she follows Johnny's instructions and performs her first clumsy movements. Then she begins to get the idea and moves more freely. Soon, Johnny is dancing intimately with her. When the music finishes, Baby does not want to stop dancing!

The following day. At the lakeside, Baby and Lisa try on wigs that make them look like Jackie Kennedy and Elizabeth Taylor in the film 'Cleopatra.'

Baby approaches Penny and tells her how much she admires Penny's dancing. Penny is evasive and hints that her life is not as glamorous as it appears to be.

Later, in the open-air pavilion, Johnny dances with Vivian Pressman. Max Kellerman describes her as a 'bungalow princess', his name for the women who live at the camp while their husbands are away on business. Vivian is a lonely woman who pays Johnny to teach her dancing. It is obvious from the way she reacts to him that she also pays Johnny for his favours.

Neil Kellerman talks romantically to Baby in the moonlight, but she wants nothing to do with him. They go to the kitchens to find something to eat. Baby spots Penny sitting on the floor in the corner, crying. She tells Billy who hurries to fetch Johnny. Johnny takes Penny back to the staff rest-room.

Penny is pregnant. We learn that Robbie, the college-boy waiter who Lisa fancies, is the father of the child. Penny will have to have an abortion or lose her job. She needs 250 dollars to pay for the operation.

Baby confronts Robbie in the dining-room next morning and asks him for the money. He refuses to have anything whatsoever to do with Penny or her problem. So Baby goes to the golf-course and asks her father for the money. She does not tell him what the money is for and lies to him when he asks if it is for anything illegal. Dr. Houseman trusts his daughter and promises to get the money for her by the evening.

Baby enters the staff disco that evening and threads her way through the embracing couples. She is excited. She has the money for Penny.

Baby interrupts Penny who is dancing with Johnny and hands her the wad of notes. Penny is taken aback. She thinks the money has come from Robbie. Then it becomes clear that Baby obtained the money from her father and Penny refuses to take it. She is made to change her mind by Johnny and Robbie.

Another problem arises. Penny can only see the doctor who will perform her operation on Thursday evening. That is the evening she is scheduled to perform the Mambo with Johnny at the nearby Sheldrake Hotel. If they fail to appear, they both lose their jobs and their summer bonus as well.

Baby offers to take Penny's place.

At first, Johnny scoffs at the idea of Baby becoming his new dancing partner. Now it is his turn to be persuaded. Penny points out what an excellent teacher Johnny is. Although reluctant, it seems the only solution.

The dancing lessons begin. Baby is a complete beginner. She feels very awkward and keeps treading on Johnny's foot.

Baby is determined to succeed. On the steps that lead to the staff quarters, she practices her movements over and over again.

The lessons continue. Baby starts to improve. Johnny explains that dancing is not just about learning the routines, you have to 'feel' the music. The beat of the Mambo is like the beat of a heart. He places Baby's hand on his heart to feel the rhythm.

Penny helps out with the instruction. The two professional dancers sandwich Baby between them as they go through the movements again and again. Then Johnny watches as Penny teaches Baby on her own. He looks pleased with Baby's progress.

36

Baby must allow herself to be led by Johnny. He tells her to watch his eyes. They will tell her what to do.

The atmosphere in the dance-lessons becomes increasingly intimate. Baby feels desire for Johnny. She aches for him to be her lover.

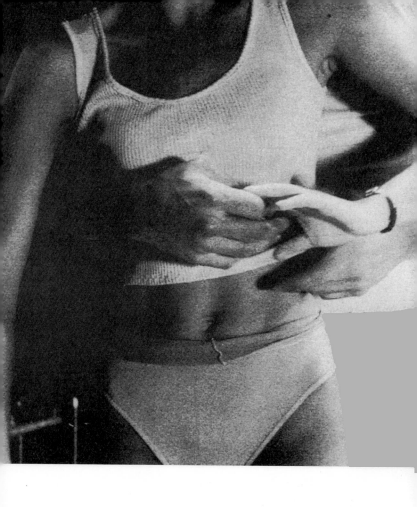

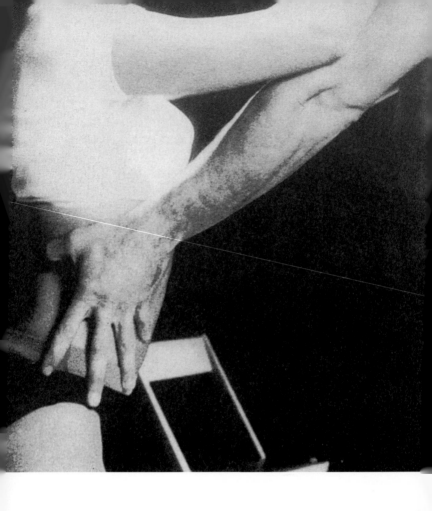

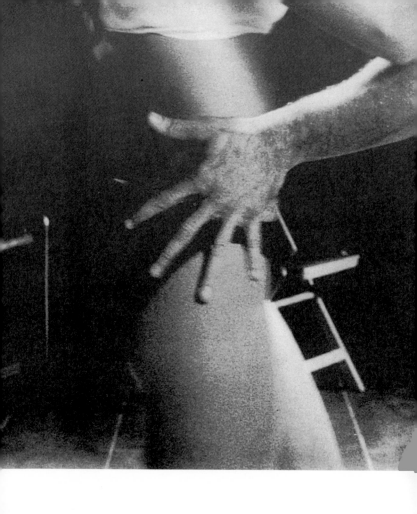

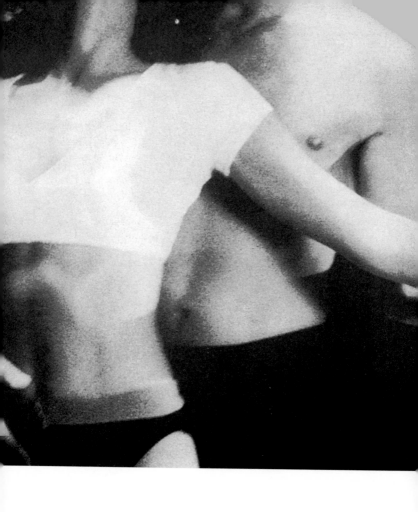

The emotional tension builds to bursting-point. Johnny is angry at Baby's mistakes and she fights back, reminding him that she is doing all this for *his* sake. The couple need a break from the dancing.

Johnny has locked his keys in his car, so he breaks the window to get in. He drives Baby out into the country.

On a high log across a gully, Johnny practices balancing. He invites Baby to join him. Then the couple go to a lake where they practice the 'lifts' for the Mambo because they are easier in the water. The tension between them has disappeared. Now they are relaxed and close.

Later, back at the camp, Baby tries on the dress
she will wear for her performance of the
Mambo.

Suddenly, Penny admits to being terrified of the
abortion she is about to have.

Baby comforts Penny by taking her in her arms. Baby reassures Penny that everything will be all right.

Before the performance, Baby asks her sister, Lisa, to tell their parents that Baby is in bed with a headache. They must not know she is out dancing with Johnny.

The Sheldrake Hotel. With her hair up and looking remarkably sophisticated, Baby begins the Mambo with Johnny.

There is a big audience in the hotel. Baby is nervous and makes mistakes. She does wrong turns and takes wrong steps. She also fails to do the 'lift' properly, only taking half a jump. Johnny, however, guides her through the difficult patches and the audience applaud their performance. Nobody seems to have noticed anything wrong.

Nobody notices, either, that Johnny is not dancing with his usual partner. Baby feels a pang of anxiety as she notices the elderly couple, the Schumakers, in the audience. Baby and Johnny finish their dance with a flourish and escape without being recognised.

Baby has been a success. Johnny praises her as they drive back to Kellerman's. Baby changes her clothes on the back seat of the car. A loving relationship has developed between the couple. They get out of the car, holding hands.

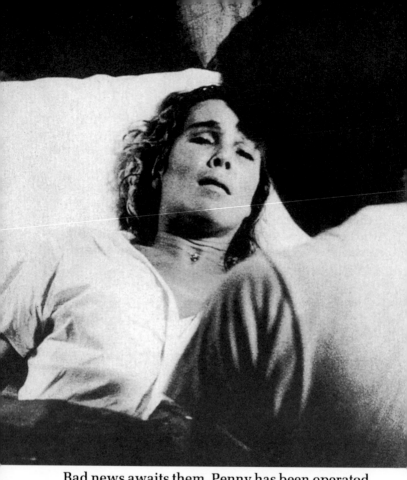

Bad news awaits them. Penny has been operated on by a fake doctor. He used a dirty knife and no anaesthetic. Penny lies in her room in great pain.

Without hesitation, Baby fetches her father. Dr. Houseman is asleep, but he senses something is seriously wrong and follows his daughter without question. He gives Penny a life-saving injection.

Dr. Houseman asks who is responsible for Penny. Johnny says he is. Johnny means that he is the closest person to Penny, but Dr. Houseman takes this to mean that Johnny is the father of Penny's baby. Dr. Houseman refuses to shake hands with Johnny when the dancer thanks him for his help. He forbids Baby to associate with people like Johnny and Penny ever again.

Baby defies her father. She goes to Johnny's room to apologise for the way Dr. Houseman treated Johnny. During the visit, Baby declares her love for Johhny. The couple dance together and Baby performs the actions of Dirty Dancing. The mimed act of love leads on to a real act of love. This is Baby's sexual awakening. Now she knows the great secret of the adult world. She has become a woman.

74

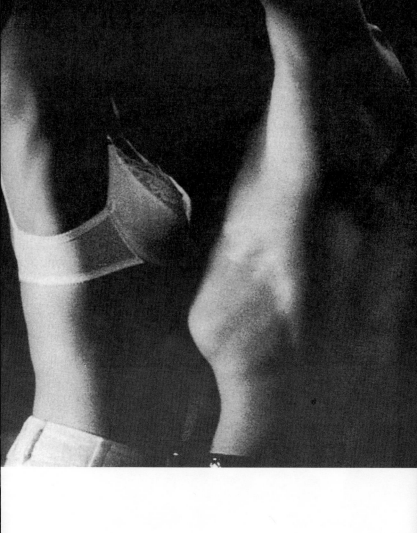

76

Breakfast the following morning. Baby sips her orange juice and stares in horror at her father who announces the family will be leaving the holiday camp. He wants to remove Baby from the bad company she is keeping.

His wife and Lisa talk their father out of his decision. Mrs Houseman points out that they have paid for their holiday in advance and Lisa is bursting to take part in the end-of-season show. She is practising a song-and-dance routine.

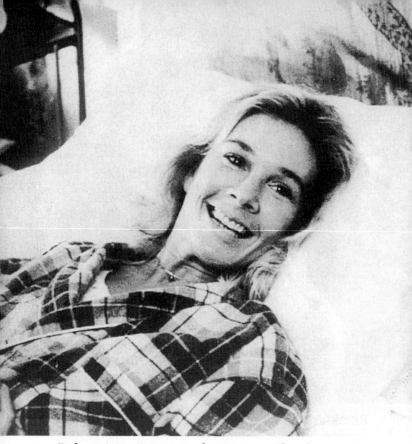

Baby visits Penny in her room. The dancer is feeling much better and should make a full recovery. Despite the abortion, Penny should be able to have children in the future.

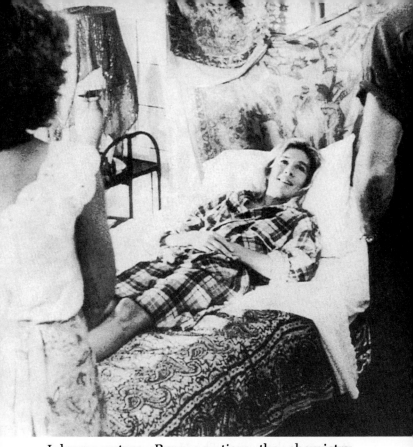

Johnny enters. Penny notices the chemistry between them. When Baby leaves, Penny urges Johnny to break off the relationship. He will lose his job if he has an affair with one of the paying guests.

Outside Penny's room, Johnny acts cool with Baby. But it only lasts a moment. Baby calls out to him and his face breaks out into a loving smile.

It rains at the camp. The Housemans are bored. Baby leaves the family chalet to visit Johnny in his room. They go to bed and make love again.

After making love, Baby wants to know if Johnny has had many women. He refuses to answer directly, but goes on to explain the predicament in which he finds himself. Rich women find him attractive and shower him with gifts. It is hard to refuse them. He is not using them: *they* are using *him*. Baby understands and gives him another loving kiss.

Then Johnny asks Baby's real name. She tells him it is Francis.

Later, Baby returns to her chalet. That night, Lisa tells her that she intends to sleep with Robbie. Knowing his secret, Baby advises her sister against it.

The following morning, the rain has stopped and the camp is back in action. Penny, now fully recovered, is back at work. We see her teaching the holidaymakers an energetic game.

Meanwhile, in the mirrored ballroom, Baby and
Johnny are dancing together. They mime to a
pop record and Baby teases her new lover by
keeping him at a distance. She reminds him of
the rule about a person's 'dance-space' that he
taught her earlier.

Neil Kellerman arrives. He is in charge of the end-of-season concert and he tells Johnny to put on an old-fashion dance. Johnny has his own ideas, but Neil Kellerman does not want to listen to them. He threatens Johnny with the sack if he does not do what he is told.

Johnny is angry. He seems to count for nothing.
As Baby walks round the camp with him,
Johnny explains how powerless he feels against
the bosses of the world who tell him what to do,
even when they are wrong. Baby argues that he
should stand up to the bosses and *make* them
listen. Johnny cannot accept this. He has never
received sympathetic treatment from anyone in
his life.

Then Baby and Johnny spot Lisa, walking past with Robbie and her father. The lovers have to hide. Johnny accuses Baby of having no intention of introducing *him* to their family. He is not a college boy like Robbie. He is not good enough for the Housemans.

Johnny walks off in a huff

Baby cannot bear to be on bad terms with Johnny. She goes to find him and they make up on the verandah of Penny's chalet. Robbie sees them and accuses Baby of 'slumming'.

This is too much for Johnny. A fight ensues. Johnny is far the stronger and Robbie is knocked to the ground. The waiter crawls away, humiliated.

Rehearsals for the end-of-season show begin. Baby is painting scenery in the background as Vivian asks Johnny to light her cigarette for her. Her husband offers Johnny money for more dancing lessons for his wife. This time, Johnny refuses. Baby allows herself a quiet smile of satisfaction. She knows that Johnny belongs to her now.

That night, Lisa goes to Robbie's room, all set to make love. She finds the student in bed with Vivian. Lisa recoils from the door, shocked and upset. Her ideal has been shattered.

Meanwhile, in Johnny's room, the two true lovers are also in bed together. Johnny tells Baby of a dream he had in which Dr. Houseman put his arm round Johnny's shoulder, just as he had seen Baby's father doing to Robbie. Baby realises how important it is for Johnny to feel himself socially acceptable.

Early next morning, Baby leaves Johnny's chalet and is spotted by Vivian as she leaves Robbie's. Vivian feels jealous that her former lover has been taken away by a mere girl. She plots revenge.

Vivian soon gets her chance. Her husband's wallet has been stolen. Vivian accuses Johnny of the crime. Not wanting to reveal that he spent the night with Baby, Johnny has no alibi. At breakfast, Max Kellerman is all set to fire the dancer. Baby cannot allow this to happen. She reveals that Johnny must be innocent because *she* spent the night with him.

The news shocks everyone, especially Baby's father. Dr. Houseman reacts by being silent and withdrawn. He feels betrayed by his daughter. She has lied to him and deceived him. Baby stands up for herself by saying that he has deceived *her*, too. He had always said that everyone was equal and deserved a fair chance in the world. Her involvement with Johnny has made her realise this is not true. Dr. Houseman was only talking of people in their own social class.

Baby goes on to apologise for deceiving her father, but she says he cannot treat her as if she was not there any more. She says she still loves her father. Then she leaves.

Dr. Houseman says nothing. He just sits with tears brimming up in his eyes.

Baby hides in the room where she first learned to dance with Johnny. Eventually, he finds her there. He has good news: Baby's suspicions were correct – the wallets *were* stolen by the Schumakers. The old couple are known criminals, wanted for theft in Florida and Arizona as well.

However, Baby's lover has still lost his job. His love-affair with Baby is now public knowledge and he has been fired because of it.

Baby is heartbroken. All her hard-work and sacrifices seem to have been in vain. Johnny disagrees. Baby's concern for his welfare has touched him deeply. Nobody has ever done anything like this for him before.

Before he leaves the camp, Johnny goes to see Dr. Houseman. He tries to explain that Baby is nothing like Dr. Houseman thinks she is. Baby's father reacts angrily to Johnny's visit and the dancer does not get a chance to explain himself or to clear up this misunderstanding about Penny's pregnancy.

Baby and Johnny part company. They exchange a few, meaningless pleasantries beside Johnny's car. A final embrace and Baby watches her lover drive away and disappear down the bumpy road in a cloud of dust.

The following days are desolate for Baby. Life has no meaning any more. She wanders aimlessly round the camp, deep in thought.

Lisa notices her sister's pain and is sympathetic. She too is suffering the effects of an unsuccessful love affair. She offers to do Baby's hair and the sisters embrace. They are reconciled after the conflict and jealousies of recent days.

The end-of-season show takes place on the last evening of the holiday. Baby sits in a dark corner with her parents. She is hardly watching the show.

Neil Kellerman leads the chorus as they sing a sentimental anthem about the summer season and the coming autumn. Baby manages a smile as Lisa completes her song-and-dance routine without mishap.

Robbie passes the table and Dr. Houseman gets up to give Robbie a cheque to enable him to continue with his medical studies. Robbie lets slip, however, that he was responsible for making Penny pregnant. Dr. Houseman is angry and disgusted. He takes back his cheque and returns to his seat.

The show is banal and boring. Then, suddenly, everything changes. Johnny returns! He enters the back of the hall, to the delight of his fellow dancers, and crosses to Baby's table. Her face lights up as she sees him and he takes her hand as he leads her towards the stage. Dr. Houseman goes to stop him, but is told to sit down by his wife.

Johnny mounts the stage and goes to the microphone. The show stops. Johnny says:

"Sorry about the disruption, folks, but I always do the last dance of the season. This year, somebody told me not to, so I'm going to do my kind of dancing with a great partner, who's not only a terrific dancer, but someone who's taught me that there are people willing to stand up for other people, no matter what it costs them. Somebody who taught me about the kind of person I want to be – Miss Francis Houseman."

Dr. Houseman and his wife watch in amazement as Johnny and Baby begin to dance the Mambo together. They had no idea that their daughter was capable of anything like this.

The couple on the stage look stunning, Baby in her pink Sweetheart dress and Johnny in tight black trousers and a black silk shirt.

Johnny and Baby dance the routines they have been practising together during the holiday. At the Sheldrake Hotel, they made mistakes. This time the performance goes perfectly. As the couple twist and twirl, the Dirty Dancers in the background shout and whistle their approval.

Johnny leaps off the stage and dances down the aisle, inviting his fellow-dancers to join in. As they advance rhythmically towards the stage, Johnny encourages Baby to do the 'lift'. The difficult and dangerous move goes without hitch and he stands holding Baby aloft like a flying bird.

The mood of excitement and emotion is infectious. The Dirty Dancers throw back the chairs and invite the members of the audience to join in. Everyone except Vivian, who leaves in disgust, joins in the joyful dance. We see Penny dancing with Dr. Houseman, two fat ladies casting caution to the wind and throwing their mink stoles to the floor, and Mrs Houseman reveals herself to be a lively mover as she dances hip-to-hip with Neil Kellerman.

Max Kellerman is astounded by the scene. He asks Tito, the band leader, if he has sheet-music for this abandoned music and dance!

Meanwhile, Johnny is reconciled with Dr. Houseman who apologises for the misunderstanding about Penny's pregnancy. Then it is Baby's turn to be reunited with her father. He tells her she looked wonderful up there on stage and she responds by giving him a loving hug.

At the end, everyone – even Max Kellerman – is joining in the dancing. The spotlight picks out Baby and Johnny, tenderly kissing. They are dancing the dance of their lives.

PART 2: COLOUR SECTION
THE CLIMAX OF THE FILM

Dirty Dancing

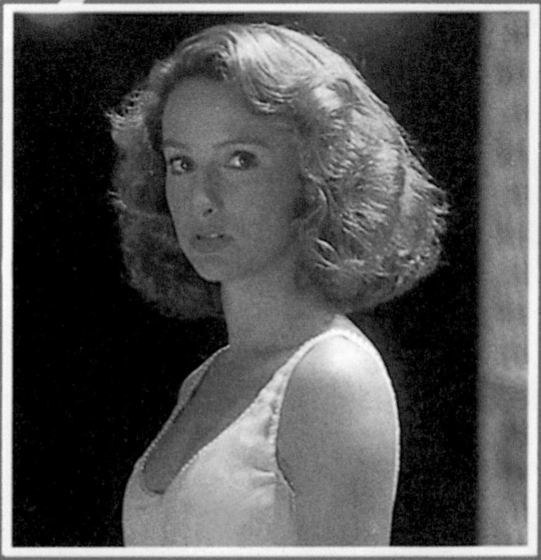

PART 3: THE BACKGROUND
TO THE FILM

CHAPTER 1. THE TIME : 1963

The choice of 1963 as the setting for 'Dirty Dancing' is an interesting one. The film is about the loss of innocence. Baby Houseman enters Kellerman's as a girl and leaves it as a woman. This growing-up process takes place against a historical background in which something similar is happening. In the summer of 1963, the world itself was about to 'grow up' too.

At the very beginning of the film, just after the opening credits, we see Baby sitting in the back of the family car on her way to the holiday camp. She mentions two events that had not yet happened. The summer of 1963 was 'before President Kennedy was shot' and 'before the Beatles'. Both these events were major turning points in the life of the times. Kennedy's assassination and the advent of the Beatles brought the world forward into a new era. After them, nothing was ever quite the same again.

We have now become accustomed to political violence. We have seen many Presidents and Prime Ministers removed from office by the bullet or the bomb. President

Kennedy's assassination was the first of modern times. Its impact was enormous : the *unthinkable* had happened. Nearly everyone who was alive at the time can remember what they were doing on that dreadful November day when the news came through. The world was stunned into disbelief. We had lost the man who seemed to promise a new future.

The early 1960s were years of hope. On both sides of the Atlantic, Youth seemed to be coming to the fore. President Kennedy was a *young* President. He was good-looking. He spoke idealistically. "Don't ask what your country can do for you." he said. "Ask what you can do for your country." (A speech which Robbie, the waiter, parodies when flirting with Lisa. "Don't ask what your waiter can do for you." he grins. "Ask what you can do for your waiter.") He stood for liberal policies of social equality and racial integration. In this country, the tired Tory government of 13 years standing was crumbling under their own scandals and the attacks of new satirical TV programmes like 'That Was The Week That Was'. Harold Wilson took over Number 10 with a massive majority. So it seemed the old order was being replaced by the new. "The Times, They Are A-Changin'." sang Bob Dylan. There was a new world just round the corner.

Then, suddenly, it was all dashed. Lee Harvey Oswald lay in wait for President Kennedy on that fateful day in Dallas. A couple of bullets and

150

PRESIDENT
JOHN F. KENNEDY

Rex Features Limited

the main focus of the world's dream was gone. Kennedy was replaced by Lyndon Johnson, a much older man who lacked Kennedy's flair and charisma. America seemed to have been suddenly thrown back to the leadership style of the 50s. And the whole world took a backwards step on November 22, 1963. Its innocence had been shattered.

The world was also changed by the arrival of the Beatles. Kennedy's assassination stood the political world on its head and the Beatles stood the entertainment world on its head. They heralded the arrival of mass Youth Culture. This began, of course, in the mid-1950s with the advent of Rock and Roll. The Beatles, however, revolutionised the world of the Young. Now they had a complete culture of their own. With the Beatles came, not only new music, but also new fashions, hairstyles, and language. Their influence led to world-wide mass movements in the mid-60s, like 'Psychedelia' and 'Flower Power'. This was something new. Nothing like it had been known before.

This is not the sort of world we see in 'Dirty Dancing'. Lisa and Baby are the last of the generation who go on holiday with their parents. At Kellerman's, they are expected to learn the same dances as their parents. The song Lisa chooses to sing at the end-of-season concert is corny and old-fashioned. The concert itself is like something put on by a school. The atmosphere at Kellerman's is dated. Looking

THE BEATLES   Rex Features Limited

153

back, Baby sees this as another aspect of her childhood she left behind in the summer of 1963.

Baby also mentions her intention of joining the Peace Corps. This organisation was set up by the U.S. Government in 1961. It was peopled by volunteers, usually school-leavers, who went abroad to help in under-developed countries. The idea was to provide expertise and manpower in education, agriculture, health, trade and technology ETC. The scheme was very popular in the early Sixties. There were 900 volunteers serving in 16 countries in 1961. By 1966 there were over 10,000 helping out in 52 countries around the world.

Volunteers were paid very little for their one or two years abroad. The idea of serving the less fortunate was very appealing to well-off American youngsters whose expensive education had made them aware of their privileged position. Telling us that Baby 'couldn't wait to join the Peace Corps', right at the beginning of the film, instantly sets her character as an idealistic youngster. She goes to Kellerman, bursting to be of service to her fellow man. Then she meets Johnny and his emotional inadequacy becomes the focus of her attention. Throughout the film, Baby is seen 'doing good', and as a result she wins Johnny's love. Baby arrives with the notion of wanting to 'change the world'. Instead, she ends up changing the self-image of another person.

154

The other aspect of 'Dirty Dancing' which needs to be put in its historical context is Penny's abortion. The film, perhaps quite rightly, does not dwell on this problem because, essentially, it is a plot device for getting Penny out of the way and allowing Baby to become Johnny's dancing partner. However, the characters expend a good deal of anguish over the matter of the abortion and this is not because they feel any moral scruples about it. It is because, 25 years ago, an unwanted pregnancy was a social disgrace that could cause a woman to lose her job, and because abortion was illegal.

In 1963, the 'Swinging Sixties' had not yet really started. The Pill had not become widely available and Sex Education did not have the high priority it has today in schools. As a result, many teenagers entered their first relationships with the opposite sex in ignorance and the girls often ended up pregnant. The social stigma attached to this was enormous, and families (particularly middle-class families) faced ostracism and disgrace if their daughters conceived out of wedlock. Penny's problem, in 'Dirty Dancing', is that she will lose her job if the news gets out. So she, like an unknown number of others, is forced to endure a 'backstreet abortion'.

Abortion was a criminal offence up until the end of the decade. Dr. Houseman's first question, when Baby asks him for 250 dollars on the golf-course, is :

"It's not for anything illegal, is it?"
Penny goes to see a travelling doctor who professes to be a real medical practitioner, but he is a brutal quack who performs the operation in a back room without any anaesthetic. Penny returns in great pain and in danger of losing her life. Then Baby intercedes on her behalf and Dr. Houseman saves her. Others, in real life, were not so fortunate. The back street abortionists led to the death or infertility of many desperate young girls.

CHAPTER 2.
THE PLACE : KELLERMAN'S
MOUNTAIN HOUSE

At the end of 'Dirty Dancing', as he stands in the wings with Tito, the band-leader, watching the end-of-season concert, Max Kellerman voices his fears for the future of his camp and the sort of holiday it provides. He says :

"I've seen it all, Tito. Serving the first campers with pasteurised milk, through the war years when we didn't have any meat, through the Depression when we didn't have anything."
He goes on :
"It isn't so much the changes, Tito. It's just that it all seems to be ending. You'd think the kids would want to come on holiday with their parents and learn the fox-trot. Fox-trot? Trips to Europe, that's what they want. 22 countries in 3 days . . .
It feels like it's all slipping away."

His words are prophetic. We know now, with the benefit of hindsight, that American holiday camps like Kellerman's lost their popularity as the decade progressed, in much the same way that Butlins and Warners went into a decline here in the early 1970s. So what is the significance of this? It continues the idea, suggested by the choice of 1963, that everything is about to change. The world is poised on the brink of a new era, and the place where Baby meets Johnny is an old-fashioned institution enjoying its final, golden swan-song. Kellerman's camp represents the world of childhood that Baby is about to leave behind.

The purpose of Kellerman's is to provide a *family* holiday.

Max Kellerman himself states this early on when Baby overhears him telling his employees how to behave. He says:
"I shouldn't have to remind you. This is a family place."

The organisation of the camp bears this out. The place offers sports and amusements by day and wholesome entertainment such as variety shows and ballroom dancing by night. The 'family feel' of the camp is highlighted by its essentially Jewish nature. Although nothing is ever stated, Kellerman's is a very Jewish place. Max Kellerman is almost a caricature of the fat, wealthy Jewish business man with his cigar and blood-pressure who exercises total personal control over his empire. The camp comedian tells a very Jewish joke about this girlfriend and his mother and, later, his voice is heard by the lakeside announcing an education class to be held by a rabbi. The names are also very Jewish –

Houseman, Pressman, the Schumakers. Vivian, the 'bungalow princess', has the long, aqualine nose and dark features of many Jewish women. And Neil Kellerman's boast to Baby about taking the lifeguard's girl because he owns 'two hotels' is a very Jewish story. Now it is well-known that Jewish people live in tight-knit communities : 'the family' is of enormous importance in their lives. So Kellerman's is where they come for the summer. The camp is designed to cater for their needs. The family atmosphere makes them feel at home.

The entertainment provided at the camp is very old-fashioned. Throughout the film, we get glimpses of the sort of amusements provided at Kellerman's – volleyball ; bingo ; golf ; playing cards ; horseshoe-throwing competitions. (We even see Penny getting the campers to jump around like kangaroos.) These are established pastimes which the camp offers its customers year after year. Similarly, the ballrooms and concert halls where the campers go in the evening have a dated, 'show-biz' air about them. The mirrored bathroom, the open-air dancefloor beside the lake with its 'Tivoli gardens' coloured lanterns and the neighbouring Sheldrake hotel with its projecting stage are well-established venues for music and entertainment whose roots are in the 1940s and 50s.

Baby quickly leaves this world behind. Being asked to take part in the first show and being sawn in half in front of an audience is an embarrassing experience for her. She escapes into the night air, blowing out her cheeks with relief. Soon, she is drawn to the staff dancefloor where she encounters Dirty Dancing for the first time. This is a completely different world. The music here is modern and the people dancing to it are adults, behaving in an adult way. As Baby enters the room, she leaves the world of childhood behind. She literally 'crosses the threshold' from girlhood to womanhood as she joins the Dirty Dancers and starts to learn their movements. There is no going back now. From this point on, Baby has almost nothing to do with the activities provided by the camp. She has her own interests to pursue.

As well as crossing from childhood to maturity during her stay at Kellerman's, Baby is also seen to cross another barrier at the camp – that of class. There are three clearly defined groups at Kellerman's. There are the paying guests whose needs are paramount. There are the college boys like Robbie who are university students employed for the summer holidays, and then there is the camp staff represented by Johnny and Penny. The first two groups are wealthy, middle-class people and Max Kellerman makes it clear that he doesn't mind them mixing. Again in the speech that Baby overhears, he says to the college boys:

"You keep your fingers out of the water, your hair out of the soup and show the goddam daughters a good time. ALL the daughters. Even the dogs (unattractive ones). Schlep them out to the terrace. Show them the stars. Romance them any way you want . . ."

Then Johnny and his dancers enter and Kellerman's tone changes. Relationships between this group and the guests is definitely *not* allowed. Wagging his stubby finger in Johnny's face, Kellerman says:

"Listen, wiseguy. You have you own rules. Dance with the daughters. Teach them the Mambo, cha-cha, anything they pay for. But that's it. That's where it ends. No funny business. No conversations. And KEEP YOUR HANDS OFF!"

There is no mistaking the great divide between the guests and the entertainment staff. Yet Baby breaks this down. She falls in love with Johnny and makes him fall in love with her. The short-term results are disastrous for them both. Baby alienates herself from her family, particularly her father, and Johnny loses his job and has to leave the camp altogether. But true love and dance conquer all. Johnny returns, takes Baby's hand and they dance the dance of their lives in front of everyone. The emotion of the occasion draws everyone in. At the end of the film, there are no differences of class because everyone is dancing together – management, staff and guests. It is a joyful climax. We feel that love has conquered prejudice and dance is a force that unites us all.

CHAPTER 3. THE MUSIC

The music of 'Dirty Dancing' is a clever mixture of old and new. Of the 25 songs that feature on the soundtrack of the film, about 15 are original songs of the 60s. The rest, including the theme song, '(I've Had) The Time Of My Life', were written recently. One would expect a significant difference in sound quality between the two, but the 'oldies' were cunningly remixed to bring them up to the musical standard of the 80s.

Many of the songs only feature for the briefest of time. They are no more than snatches of music in the background, lending atmosphere and helping to give a feel of the time. Others, however, play a much more important part in the film. They help to tell the story. The words of the songs, and the style of the music, tell us how the characters are feeling at the time. When this is happening, we usually hear a lot more of the song.

'Dirty Dancing' begins with the whole of 'Be My Baby', sung by the Ronettes. The song is accompanied by a black and white version of the dirty dancing scene we see later on. It is also slowed down visually and slightly blurred. Both devices are very effective. The black and white gives a 'documentary' feel to the opening credits. It is like watching a newsreel of the 60s. The slowed-down/blurred effect gives the sequence a dreamlike quality that is mysterious and exciting. The choice of 'Be My Baby' is also significant. The song is very vibrant and hits us right between the eyes from the very first moment the film begins. It is also very evocative of 1963. At this time, Phil Spector's music was at the height of its popularity. Known as Phil Spector's 'wall of sound', it usually featured a black singing group accompanied by a very heavy musical background. And the words of the song have a direct bearing on the story that is about to unfold. The Ronettes ask that someone become their baby. The name of the central character is 'Baby'. We are about to see her fall in love with Johnny. She becomes *his* baby.

After this punchy opening sequence, we are given no respite. The soundtrack immediately fades into the voice of Cousin Bruce Morrow, the 60s disc-jockey, enthusing about the summer ahead. He says it is the time for romance when EVERYONE is in love. Then we go straight into 'Big Girls Don't Cry' by Frankie Valli and The Four Seasons. It sounds a warning that the romances ahead for the two girls we see sitting in the car are not going to be easy. Both Baby and Lisa are made miserable by their love-affairs and, at the end of the summer, only Baby has found true love. Lisa ends up with nothing.

We hear no more songs for a while now. Music takes over as the film unfolds. The Merengue music for Penny's dancing class in the open-air ballroom is a modern composition, written and performed by Michael Lloyd who has a hand in all the new contributions to the soundtrack. We then get a brief snatch of the love-theme, '(I've Had) The Time Of My Life', as Baby goes to look round the camp. It suggests that something important is about to happen and is followed by Baby's first glimpse of Johnny in the dining-room. Big band music cuts in next. It is the first ballroom scene with Tito, the bandleader, doing his little tap-dance and being joined by Max Kellerman for their duet. This music pin-points the old-fashioned nature of the holiday camp's entertainment. This is 1940s-style music with whole families, including precocious children like the ones who push past Baby, on the dancefloor. This dance-band music suddenly gives way to the Mambo. Penny and Johnny appear and take over the floor with their stunning display of Mambo dancing. The music they dance to is called 'Johnny's Mambo' and is another Michael Lloyd production from 1987.

As Baby escapes from the camp comedian whose tedious jokes embarrass her, music is heard coming from the staff quarters in the distance. It is modern, pop music and it beckons to her like a siren. She enters the staff dancefloor with Billy and, as the doors open, the sound of 'Do You Love Me?' by the Contours blares out at us at full volume. This is the longest song-sequence in the film. It is also the most important scene. Baby encounters Dirty Dancing for the first time. She is invited to join in by Johnny and finds herself enjoying it. All the time this action is going on, we hear The Contours asking for love as a result of learning to dance. Nothing could be more appropriate. Baby is starting to do both. The record changes near the end of this scene and we hear 'Love Man', by Otis Redding. This is when Baby is dancing close to Johnny and allowing him a considerable amount of physical contact with her. The song is also very apt. She sees Johnny at this point as an object of desire. He is her 'Love Man.'

There is a brief interlude of ballroom music when Johnny is seen dancing with Vivian, then we are back to more Dirty Dancing. Baby returns with the 250 dollars she has procured for Penny's operation. This time the music playing is 'Stay' by Maurice Williams and the Zodiacs. The words of the song are like an echo of Baby's thoughts. They ask that she should remain a little while longer and prolong the moment of togetherness by having a further dance. This is Baby's dream. She has set her heart on Johnny and wants his love. To stay with Johnny and dance is what Baby wants to do more than anything else in the world.

Then she gets her chance. Baby replaces Penny as Johnny's partner. We hear some ballroom music on the gramophone as we see Baby's plimsolled feet repeatedly stepping on Johnny's toes. This music is quickly replaced by the frantic beat of 'Wipe Out' by The Sufaris, and we see Baby practicing her movements on the steps to the staff quarters. The staccato rhythm of this song is just right to express Baby's vexation at not being able to master the movements: she positively *dances* with frustration at her constant mistakes. She knows, to get Johnny, she must master the Mambo. Otherwise she faces a 'wipe-out' – a term from surfing which describes being knocked sideways off your board. It means total failure.

The long sequence of dancing lessons has now started. During it, the hit songs come thick and fast. The heartbeat scene, where Johnny holds Baby's hand to his heart to feel the rhythm, fades into the beginning of 'Hungry Eyes' by Eric Carmen. This wonderful song provides the music by which Penny, Johnny and Baby dance as a threesome. Eyes are all important here. Johnny points emphatically at his eyes, urging Baby to watch them so he can lead her in the dance. Wearing the briefest of dancewear, she gazes back at him with intense passion. The lyrics say it all. They express extreme desire and determination to win a lover. Love is seen as a hunger gaining expression through the eyes. Eric Carmen's high, haunting voice spells out Baby's resolution to take possession of Johnny now that he is within her grasp. The music continues as Baby and Johnny practice the most erotic movement of the Mamba where his hand traces the outline of her shape. At first, Baby giggles like a schoolgirl. But the third and forth time, she responds as if she is being caressed. The dancing has stopped for a moment. Her desire is positively visible.

The atmosphere becomes too much and the couple quarrel. The musical accompaniment to this is 'Overload' by Zappacosta. The term is suggestive of electricity and is very apt to describe their emotional relationship at this point. There is *too much* feeing between them. They need a break.

So Johnny takes Baby out into the country. It is indicative of the tension they are feeling that he is prepared to smash the window of his car in order to get the keys which he has locked in. Once out in the open air, the harmony between the couple is restored. Johnny practices balancing on a high log and invites Baby to join him. As he holds out his hand, we hear 'Hey, Baby' by Bruce Channel. This song marks something of a turning-point. It is the first time that Johnny has asked Baby to be *his* lover. Before, it has always been the other way round.

The 'lifts' scene in the lake is accompanied by the instrumental version of the love-theme, '(I've Had) The Time Of My Life'. Combined with the joyous splashing of the couple in the lake and the romantic pink of the sky, this delightful tune leaves us in no doubt that Johnny has fallen for Baby and the two of them are becoming lovers.

The Mambo music during the performance at the Sheldrake Hotel gives way to a song on the car radio on the way home. The disc-jockey announces The Drifters singing 'Some Kind of Wonderful', a lesser-known hit from the famous song-writing team of Carole King and Gerry Goffin. We only hear a few lines of the song, but they are played as Johnny praises Baby for her performance and confirm that he is feeling admiration and affection for his plucky young dancing partner. The Drifters, with their delicate harmonies, sing about tender feelings that have taken them by surprise. The couple return to Kellerman's, holding hands.

The musical accompaniment to the first love scene in Johnny's room is 'Cry To Me' by Soloman Burke. The choice of the song is very clever. The words suggest the idea of abandonment. Burke's raspy voice asks for all emotions to be surrendered to him.

This is just what Baby is doing. She declares her love for Johnny and then abandons herself to him. It is also clever the way in which Baby performs a Dirty Dancing movement to suggest the physical relationship that is about to happen. Johnny holds her and she leans backwards, languorously sweeping her head in a circle. This sort of suggestive movement shocked Baby only a few days earlier. Now she is doing them herself and it seems quite natural.

The second love-scene, on the wet afternoon, is

followed by a long section of "Will You Love Me Tomorrow?" by The Shirelles. This is another Goffin and King composition from 1960. The words express Baby's doubt about her new lover. They ask questions about his fidelity. Is this going to be a lasting relationship or just a brief, sexual affair? Having made love more than once now, Baby is thinking of the future and hoping this could be permanent.

Baby asks Johnny if he's had many women. He doesn't answer her directly, but explains that he feels 'used' by rich women such as Vivian who want him because they are lonely and bored. Baby is satisfied with this explanation and kisses him affectionately.

By the time we reach the scene in the mirrored ballroom, Baby has become a confident lover, able to tease her partner. Baby and Johnny mime the words and actions to the song 'Love Is Strange' by Mickey and Sylvia. Johnny is seen trying to get his hands on Baby and, in the song, it is the man who is asking the questions of the girl. He wants to know how she summons her lover and the girl's answer is that she just calls to him and he comes running. Visually, Baby accompanies this song by crooking her finger at Johnny and then wriggling away to hide behind a screen. Clearly, the tables have been turned. Now it is Johnny who is in pursuit of Baby and she is playfully keeping out of his reach. (She even has the nerve to throw back in Johnny's face his advice about 'dancing-space').

Johnny and Baby mime to 'Love Is Strange', by
Mickey and Sylvia

Neil Kellerman interrupts Baby's coquettish behaviour, but we are left in no doubt that she is firmly in possession of Johnny's affections.

The songs fade out of the action for a while now. They reappear as Lisa approaches Robbie's chalet with a view to making love to him. The song in the background is 'Yes' by Merry Clayton and it expresses Lisa's determination to finally take the plunge. She is all dressed up and the words of the song express excitement at a night of physical love-making ahead. But Lisa is making a mistake. Baby has already pointed out to her sister that this attitude is all wrong and Lisa gets her come-uppance when she finds Robbie in bed with Vivian. Then the attention switches to Baby and Johnny who are also in bed together. Unlike Lisa and Robbie, their love-making is motived by true feelings and so the song that accompanies this scene is a tender love-song by The Five Satins, 'In The Still Of The Night.' The words promise fidelity and a long-lasting relationship. And the idea of being together in the middle of the night suggests peace and security. This is just the opposite of how Lisa is feeling, having gone the wrong way about finding a partner. The contrast between Lisa and Baby is made crystal clear by the way in which the two scenes are juxtaposed. We actually *see* a record-player changing records. Baby's song visibly follows Lisa. Her loving relationship with Johnny is the 'flipside' of Lisa's misguided desire and Robbie's loveless fornication with Vivian.

172

When Johnny leaves, Baby feels desolate and we hear the song 'She's Like The Wind' as she moons listlessly round the camp. The song is sung by Patrick Swayze himself. He has a beautifully melodic voice and the song creates a mood of melancholy. The words suggest the idea of worthlessness. The girl in the song is beyond the reach of the singer. He is silly to think she would want anything to do with him. We know that this is exactly how Johnny feels about Baby. As she wanders through the night, it is like listening to the voice of Johnny's ghost echoing round the camp.

Then Baby has to attend the final concert. She manages a smile at her sister's solo in 'Kellerman's Anthem.' This is a modern song, written for the film, but typical of the sort of sentimental chorus with which the holiday camps closed their summer seasons. The 'hearts and hands' theme cuts no ice with the Dirty Dancers who stand at the back of the hall like cynical Fifth Formers at a school concert. The anthem is interrupted by Johnny's arrival and the song is abandonned in favour of the final, triumphant song – the vocal version of '(I've Had) The Time Of My Life'. It is interesting that this song is a duet. Bill Medley and Jennifer Warnes sing the love theme *together* and their voices are like the voices of Johnny and Penny. This is not a one-sided love affair. Baby has fallen in love with Johnny and succeeded in making him fall in love with her. It is a two-way relationship and the song that expresses it is sung by two voices.

'Dirty Dancing' closes with the whole of 'Yes' by Merry Clayton, a snatch of which we heard as Lisa approaches Robbie's chalet. As the end-credits roll over another black and white background, bringing the film full-circle, the words of the song sum everything up. They express joy and satisfaction at finding true love. The music is driving and up-tempo. The message is totally affirmative. 'Dirty Dancing' ends on a note of triumph.

THE SOUNDTRACK IN DETAIL:

'Be My Baby' by The Ronettes.
'Big Girls Don't Cry' by Frankie Valli and
The Four Seasons.
'The Merengue'.
'The Fox Trot'.
'Johnny's Mambo'.
'Where Are You Tonight?' by Tom Johnston.
'Do You Love Me?' by The Contours.
'Love Man' by Otis Redding.
'Stay' by Maurice Williams and The Zodiacs.
'Wipe Out' by The Surfaris.
'Hungry Eyes' by Eric Carmen.
'Overload' by Zappacosta.
'Hey, Baby' by Bruce Chanel.
'De Todo Un Poco' by Melon.
'Some Kind of Wonderful' by The Drifters.
'These Arms Of Mine' by Otis Redding.
'Cry To Me' by Soloman Burke.
'Will You Love Me Tomorrow?' by
The Shirelles.
'Love Is Strange' by Mickey and Sylvia.
'You Don't Own Me' by The Blow Monkeys.
'Yes' by Merry Clayton.
'In The Still Of The Night' by The Five Satins.
'She's Like The Wind' by Patrick Swayze.
'(I've Had) The Time Of My Life' by
Jennifer Warnes and Bill Medley.

CHAPTER 4. THE DANCES

The Dirty Dancing that gives this film its name is not really dancing at all. The movements stand for something else. The real dancing that takes place in 'Dirty Dancing' centres around The Mambo.

In 1963 NOBODY danced like the Dirty Dancers in that staff disco! The steps (such as they are) had not even been thought of. Dirty Dancing is a product of the late 80s. Behind it lies a long and increasingly permissive line of erotic dancing that includes musicals like 'Hair', the television dancing group 'Hot Gossip' and the choreography of erotic shows such as those staged at Raymond's Revue Bar. In 1963, the dances that even the most way-out teenagers were doing was a frantic sort of shake and bop.

The Dirty Dancing in this film is a form of mimed love-making. The movements are explictly sexual. In the first, prolonged Dirty Dancing sequence, we see the couples pressing their pelvises together; the girls pout their lips and lifts their legs; the boys make fondling movements and put their faces closes to their partners' stomachs. No intimate contact between the couples is actually seen, but everything is suggested. The overall effect is to create the atmosphere of an orgy. Baby appears to enter a den of iniquity, a fascinating new world which stands in complete contrast to the world outside. As a symbol for adult sexual passion, the Dirty Dancing works very well. We all share her fascination for this explicit eroticism. But it is very interesting that when they learn to dance together, Baby and Johnny do the Mambo and they perform the Mambo when they proclaim their relationship to the world. If Dirty Dancing represents sex in this film, Mambo dancing stands for love and true partnership.

The Mambo is a ballroom dance that originally came from Cuba. It became popular all over the world in the late 1940s. The dance is essentially a version of the Rumba which is still an established part of Latin American dancing today. The foot-patterns of the two dances are more-or-less the same, the basic movements being to step backwards, step forwards, close and hold. The main difference between the Rumba and the Mambo is that, in the Rumba, the couple tend to dance together in the standard ballroom embrace whereas, in the Mambo, the couple dance more by themselves, just holding one hand, and tend to part and come together more often. In fact, the Mambo slowly evolved into the Cha-Cha-Cha, a dance which is mentioned in 'Dirty Dancing' but not seen.

The important thing about the Mambo is that the couple have to be in perfect partnership to perform it properly. At the start of the film, Baby is a complete beginner. She has to learn the dance from scratch. To do this requires steely determination on her part and expert teaching from Johnny. Their first public performance, at the hotel, is only a partial success. Baby cannot do the lifts. Then, at the end, when Johnny returns to claim her and they dance on the stage at Kellerman's, she performs the lift successfully and Johnny holds her above his head, her arms spread out like a bird, smiling triumphantly. This last display is perfect. Baby and Johnny have 'got it right' at last. They are equal partners who understand and trust each other totally.

Then everyone take to the dancefloor and the film ends with the old and young, rich and poor, black and white all dancing together. Dance has already come to stand for sexual passion and mutual love. Now it stands for social harmony. All the conflicts have been resolved and this group of people are united in a natural and joyous activity.

CHAPTER 5. THE MAIN CHARACTERS

BABY

It has been said that the essence of drama is conflict and the essence of a good story is change. In 'Dirty Dancing' we have both. There is conflict between Baby Houseman and her father and there is her change from girl to woman through her love for Johnny.

The second theme is more important than the first and forms the emotional 'heart' of the film. When Baby arrives at Kellerman's for the start of her three-week holiday, she is still a young girl. By the time we reach the end-of-season concert, she has become a woman and proclaims this to the world through her dance with Johnny. The change is clear to see. But, in story-telling terms, how is it done? How does Emile Ardolino, the director of the film, show us the way in which the character of Baby matures?

Firstly, there is the change in her clothes. At the very beginning, Baby wears a girlish blue dress. She also wears a long, fluffy cardigan and flat shoes which give her an immature appearance. She wears this outfit right up until she becomes involved with Johnny and the Dirty Dancers. Once she has agreed to take Penny's place as Johnny's dancing-partner, everything changes. On the steps leading to the staff quarters, we see her intently practising her dance-steps. Now she is wearing a tight, red tee-shirt and blue shorts that make her look far more grown-up and sexy. There there are dance-lessons with Johnny in which she wears two-piece outfits that reveal her midriff or bikini-pants covered by dark tights. The increasingly erotic atmosphere is furthered by the sequence in the lake where the couple practise their lifts. Baby gets her clothes wet and ends up resembling a picture from a man's magazine. From here onwards she wears grown-up clothes, culminating in the beautiful, flowing pink 'sweetheart' dress she wears at the end for her final triumphant Mambo with Johnny.

The second way in which we are made to realise the development taking place in the central character is the change in Baby's name. In the opening scene, in the family car, Baby tells us her name is 'Baby'. The choice of this name is fairly blatant and leaves us in no doubt that we are supposed to think of her as a young girl. Furthermore, she gives us this information in voiceover which gives the impression she now knows better. She says:

"I was known as Baby and wasn't old enough to mind."

182

*BABY PAINTS SCENERY FOR THE
END-OF-SEASON CONCERT*

This suggests that she minds now. She is not the person she was: she has grown up. The crucial point of change, however, is the scene with Johnny after they have made love for the second time. Johnny realises he does not know Baby's real name. "Francis." she replies. "After the first women in the Cabinet". Johnny kisses her and says: "Francis. That's a real grown-up name."

The third and final way in which we are made aware of Baby's emotional progress is through her dancing. Dance stands for many things in this film – sexual desire and its fulfilment; the love between a man and a woman; a bridge between classes and generations and social unity. In terms of her dancing, Baby arrives a complete beginner and leaves a confident professional.

Baby's first dance is the Merengue in the open-air pavilion with Penny. She looks awkward, but is encouraged to join in and begins to enjoy herself. It is clear from the start that she has no dancing experience. Then she enters the staff dancefloor, carrying that huge water-melon. She looks wide-eyed and innocent, like a schoolgirl entering a brothel. Johnny picks her out and encourages her to join in. The movements they make to the music are blatantly sexual. Baby looks overawed, yet fascinated. When the music stops, Baby carries on dancing. She does not want this new experience to stop. Then Baby becomes Johnny's dancing partner and they have to learn to Mambo for the performance at the Sheldrake hotel. The learning process is difficult and painful. At one point, when Johnny is angry with her, she threatens to give up and confronts him with the fact that she is learning this dance for *his* sake. So there is a bond between them, a common purpose that unites them emotionally as well as just as dancing partners. In the log-walking sequence and the scene in the lake that follow this tiff, they act more as equals and dancing together has become fun. The splashing in the water is accompanied by laughter and followed by kissing. Dance is now a form of love-play.

The performance of the Mambo in the hotel is another turning point. Baby does well enough for the audience not to notice that she isn't Johnny's usual partner. On the way home in the car, Johnny thanks Baby and praises her performance. They get out of the car holding hands and the union seems quite natural. Later, after Dr. Houseman has seen to Penny and forbidden Baby to associate with Johnny's crowd any more, Baby returns to Johnny's room. He goes to turn his record player off, but Baby urges him to leave it on. Then she gets up, saying: "Dance with me." What she means is: "Make love to me." She gives herself to Johnny and, in the tender sequence that follows, they make love for the first time. Baby has become a woman.

The next time Baby and Johnny dance together is

in the empty, mirrored ballroom when they are interrupted by the arrival of Neil Kellerman. Before he breaks their mood, we see Baby teasingly keeping Johnny at bay. Playfully, she throws back at him all the advice he gave her about keeping to their own 'dancing space'. He is no longer her teacher. She is now his equal and they are partners in every sense of the word. We don't see them together again until the very end. With the desolation of Johnny's departure from the camp still fresh in her mind, Baby attends the end of season concert. Back with her parents, she has to sit through her sister's appalling song and dance routine and the corny, sentimental song led by Neil Kellerman. Then Johnny returns and they dance the dance of their lives. This time, there are no mistakes. The lifts, which Baby failed to do at the hotel, now go perfectly. Their dance proclaims to everyone that they are a couple, together and united. The drama and emotion of the moment is enough to convince Baby's mother that this relationship is for real and, when Dr Houseman learns of Robbie's involvement with Penny, he comes over to their side too.

The film ends with everybody dancing together. Many of Shakespeare's plays, particularly his comedies, end in the same way. The dance is a symbol of social unity that has been restored through the action of the play. Not only do Baby and Johnny proclaim their love in public through the togetherness of their dancing, the wave of emotion that this engenders sucks in the audience and everyone joins in, forgetting their conflicts and quarrels in a spontaneous display of emotion expressed through dance. (Vivian is the only one who does not join in. She is the 'baddie' and leaves in disgust.) This spontaneous dance, at the end of the film, leaves us with the impression that everyone, even the misfits, have somewhere to belong.

The conflict between Baby and her father is less well-handled in the film than Baby's triumphant progress to emotional maturity. The problem is that it is not a true conflict between Baby and Dr. Houseman because his opposition to her relationship with Johnny is based on a misunderstanding. When Baby calls him out in the middle of the night to attend to Penny, Dr. Houseman asks:

"Who's responsible for this girl?"

Johnny answers: "I am." Dr. Houseman takes this to mean that Johnny is the father of Penny's baby. In fact Johnny means that he is the person closest to Penny and is prepared to look after her. As a result of this misunderstanding, Dr. Houseman refuses to shake hands with Johnny and forbids Baby ever to associate with the Dirty Dancers again. It is not until right at the end of the film, when Robbie lets slip his liaison with Penny, that the misunderstanding is cleared up and the prejudice against Johnny is removed.

The artificial nature of the conflict between Baby

187

and her father gives the confrontation between them on the verandah of their chalet a rather limited force. Most teenage girls face parental disapproval of their first relationships, particularly in this case as it is with an older man from a different social class, clearly involving a strong sexual element. Dr. Houseman reacts to Baby's defiance of his wishes by being moody and introverted. He professes to being hurt by the lies Baby has told him. Baby counters by saying that he has lied to her, too. Her protected childhood has kept her from a true knowledge of the world. In a rather muddled speech, she says:

"You told me that everyone was equal and deserved a fair chance. But you were only speaking of people like you. Once you hoped I would change the world and make it a better place. But you expected me to do it by becoming a lawyer and marrying a graduate from Harvard."

She goes on:

"I still love you, Daddy. I'm sorry I have let you down. But you haven't told me the truth, either."

We are supposed to feel that Baby has won the argument because we leave Dr. Houseman with his eyes brimming over with tears. But the confrontation has been far from gripping. If Dr. Houseman had *really* wanted to prevent Baby from seeing Johnny again, he would have insisted on taking his family away from the camp and not allowing himself to be over-ruled by the wishes of his wife and Lisa. Furthermore, throughout the film, Baby appears to act exactly as she pleases and shows no guilt whatsoever at disobeying her father. So her apologies to him don't have a real ring of truth about them.

Most fathers feel protective towards their daughters when they grow up and start dating. Perhaps it would have been better for Dr. Houseman to have opposed Baby's liaison with Johnny because he did not want to 'let her go.' This would have fitted better with the statement at the start of the film, when Baby put her arms round her dad's neck in the car, that she was not expecting to find a 'guy who was greater than her dad.' At least, then, the conflict between father and daughter would have been natural rather than engineered. On the other hand, a strong secondary theme like this could have clouded the issue and detracted from the main thrust of the film which is to show the metamorphosis of a teenage girl into a young woman through love, sexual passion and dance.

JOHNNY

When Johnny makes his first appearance in 'Dirty Dancing', Baby is watching from behind a door. Her eyes widen with excitement and desire as he struts in, leading his team of dancers. He wears dark glasses and carries his coat over his shoulder. There are definite echoes of John Travolta in 'Saturday Night Fever' and 'Grease' in the surly way he reacts to Max Kellerman's strictures and threatens to quarrel with college-boy, Robbie. Yet, as the film progresses, we learn that Johnny's swaggering confidence is a bluff. Really, he has no self-esteem. Just as he teaches her to dance, Baby teaches him to have self-respect. The two processes go on together.

The first inkling we get that Johnny is more vulnerable than he looks is during the first Dirty Dancing scene when Baby and Johnny's cousin, Billy, watch Johnny dancing with Penny. To look at them, you would think they were a couple. But Billy explains that their relationship has finished and now they are dancing-partners only. This means Johnny is alone. He has no-one but himself. If also means that he is 'free' and Baby can become his lover.

Johnny soon finds himself in trouble. Penny is pregnant and, as her ex-lover and current dancing partner, Johnny says he is responsible for her welfare. Yet he does not have the money to procure an abortion for Penny which will save her from shame. Baby's first act is to go straight to her father and ask him for 250 dollars, even though she knows it is for something illegal and involves deceiving Dr. Houseman. Johnny is grateful to her and encourages Penny to take the money. Then, with the prospect of Penny's absence on Thursday evening when they have to dance the Mamba, Johnny is threatened with the loss of his job and his entire bonus for the season. Once again, Baby steps in. This time she offers to learn the dance and take Penny's place.

Johnny's slowly increasing respect for Baby is cleverly shown during the sequence of dance lessons. Later, when she comes to his room in immediate defiance of her father's commands, he blurts out how worthless he feels. He has no class. He has no regular income and lives his life from hand to mouth. The rich women who throw themselves at him make him think he's something important, but really they are just using him for their own purposes. Baby listens to all this and replies by saying that Johnny is *everything* because of the way he makes her feel. She is confessing her love for him. Her love is seen as the missing ingredient in Johnny's life. From now on, he can begin to feel strong.

The next big lapse in Johnny's self-image occures when Neil Kellerman interrupts their coy dance in the mirrored ballroom to instruct Johnny about the end-of-season dance. Johnny has his own ideas about this, but Neil Kellerman insists on the Petchenga, another old-fashioned dance. He threatens Johnny with the sack if he

JOHNNY IN HIS ROOM

does not obey. Baby is surprised at Johnny's subservience. As they walk round the camp together, she urges him to stand up for his ideas. Johnny retorts that it is futile to argue the bosses. They never listen. So it is easier to do what you are told. But Baby's advice sinks in and we see Johnny acting upon it when he returns at the end of the film.

In the meantime, Johnny has been accused of stealing the wallet belonging to Vivian's husband, Mr. Pressman. Once again, Baby comes to his rescue at the expense of compromising herself. She finally confesses to spending the night with Johnny, thus giving him a watertight alibi and proving he did not steal the wallet. Johnny cannot understand Baby's altruism. "Nobody," he says afterwards, "ever did anything like this for me before."

Johnny gets the sack anyway because of his involvement with Baby. The lovers part in that rather underplayed scene beside Johnny's car. Now everything is set for the big finale. During the end-of-season concert, Johnny comes back! Like Richard Gere in 'An Officer and a Gentleman', the hero returns to claim his girl. In fact, there is more to it than that. On the stage, talking into the microphone to the astonished audience, Johnny proclaims to everyone that he is no longer going to be pushed around and his new-found self-respect is all thanks to Baby. He says:

"Sorry about the disruption, folks, but I always do the last dance of the season. This year, sombody told me not to, so I'm going to do my kind of dancing with a great partner, who's not only a terrific dancer, but someone who's taught me that there are people willing to stand up for other people, no matter what it costs them. Somebody who taught me about the kind of person I want to be – Miss Francis Houseman."

This says it all. The two-way process is now complete. Johnny has taught Baby to be a woman; she has taught him to be a man.

PENNY

In 'Dirty Dancing', the character of Penny is less well-defined than that of Baby or Johnny because, as the storyline develops, her importance diminishes. Essentially, she gets out of the way in order to allow Baby and Johnny's relationship to develop, rather like a pacemaker in a running race who allows the main runners to take over the lead.

It is to Cynthia Rhodes's credit that she manages to inject some life into the character of Penny and to make her more or less believable. Her performance at the beginning of the film is vibrant and she puts some powerful emotion into the dilemma of Penny's abortion and its consequences. There is a way, too, in which Penny contributes to the 'growth and development' theme of the main storyline.

Penny hits the screen early on, flashing her skirts and shrieking excitedly as she attempts to make her Merengue dancing-class fun for the holidaymakers. We see her again soon afterwards, performing that impromptu Mambo with Johnny that the guests so love and Max Kellerman cuts short. Then she enters the Dirty Dancing den and proceeds to show that she is the mistress of the erotic dance as well as classical ballroom steps. She seems attractive, vibrant and confident.

Yet, like Johnny, Penny is a flawed masterpiece.

PENNY WITH JOHNNY AT THE LAKESIDE

She has allowed herself to become pregnant. The father is Robbie, the college boy from Yale who is only working at Kellerman's for the summer. As she explains later, she thought Robbie loved her. She also has the same, deprived background as Johnny. Her mother threw her out when she was 16 and all she knows is dancing. When, at the lakeside, Baby tells Penny how much she admires her dancing and Penny walks off without reply, we feel a whiff of bitterness at the hardness of her lot. Similarly, when Baby gives her the money for her abortion, Penny begins by refusing it. She has the fierce pride of the disadvantaged.

Just as she does with Johnny, however, Baby breaks down the barriers between her and Penny by her concern and good-nature. Penny *does* take the money for the abortion and is enthusiastic about the idea of Baby replacing her as Johnny's dancing partner. On both counts, Penny has good cause to be grateful to Baby and it is not long before we see them involved in a tender moment together. As Baby tries on Penny's red dress for the Mambo performance with Johnny, Penny suddenly confesses to feeling afraid of her forthcoming abortion. The two girls embrace, like sisters. Gone is the angry reaction that Baby is an interfering do-gooder from another social world.

After the abortion goes wrong, Baby rushes to fetch her father who saves Penny's life. When Baby visits Penny after she gets better, the

197

atmosphere is almost loving between the two girls, Baby smiling down kindly on Penny who beams as she says she will make a full recovery. Then Johnny arrives and Penny notices the emotion between them. Penny's last act, before she fades out of the action of the film until almost the very end, is to warn Johnny off Baby. Her concern is for him. He will lose his job if he remains emotionally involved with one of the guests. Penny's advice does not last long. Johnny can only stay cool with Baby for a few moments. She calls his name and his love for her shows on his face.

Penny does not appear again until she joins in with the joyful community dancing just before the closing credits. She has done her job, highlighting the qualities in Baby, the heroine, and making way for her to take possession of the hero.

CHAPTER 6
THE STARS OF THE FILM
PATRICK SWAYZE

'Dirty Dancing' proved to be a turning point in Patrick Swayze's film career. Before his performance as Johnny Castle, the handsome young actor and dancer had appeared in a small number of films including Francis Ford Coppola's 'The Outsiders' and the overtly political 'The Red Flood', but was best known for his part in the TV mini-series 'North and South'. After the runaway success of 'Dirty Dancing', he became a household name all over the world and a Hollywood superstar with millions of swooning female fans.

Born on August 18, 1952, in Houston, Texas (and claiming to be part Apache Native American), Patrick came from a performing arts background. His mother, Patsy Swayze, was a choreographer who ran a dancing school and the young Swayze received formal ballet training at two famous schools in New York until problems with his knees forced him to switch from dancing to acting.

Even greater film success followed hard on the heels of 'Dirty Dancing'. Three years later, in 1990, Swayze starred as Sam Wheat in 'Ghost'. The scene in which the spectral lover leans over the shoulder of Demi Moore, tenderly helping her to mould a clay pot, has gone down in cinema history as one of everyone's all-time favourite moments. Then in 1991 came the role of Bodhi in 'Point Break', one of the criminal surfers in this breathtaking thriller.

Ever since 1975, Patrick Swayze has been married to Lisa Niemi. The couple met at his mother's dancing school when Lisa was only 15 and they have been together ever since. They own ranches in California and New Mexico where they breed Arabian horses.

This idyllic refuge came into its own in the early Nineties when the actor, now a well-established Hollywood name making more than one film a year, suffered a breakdown. It was triggered by the suicide of his sister Vicky in 1994 and led Swayze to be admitted to a clinic for alcoholism. He recovered and retreated to his ranches to recuperate, returning to the silver screen in triumph in 1995 with a Golden Globe nomination for his role as Vida Boheme in 'To Wong Foo, Thanks for Everything! Julie Newmar'.

Despite his long-term marriage and huge financial success, Patrick Swayze has always been looking for something else from life. He was brought up a Roman Catholic, but left that faith to become a Baptist, a Buddhist and a Scientologist. He remains a deeply spiritual person with a strong belief in the healing power of crystals.

Everything went full-circle in 2004 when he returned to 'Dirty Dancing', playing a cameo role as a dance instructor in the updated sequel called 'Dirty Dancing: Havana Nights'.

*PATRICK SWAYZE
IN 'NORTH AND SOUTH'*

Filmography

(From 'Dirty Dancing' onwards)

1987	'Dirty Dancing' (Johnny Castle)
1987	'Steel Dawn' (Nomad)
1988	'Tiger Warsaw' (Chuck 'Tiger' Warsaw)
1989	'Road House' (James Dalton)
1989	'Next Of Kin' (Truman Gates)
1990	'Ghost' (Sam Wheat)
1991	'Point Break' (Bodhi)
1992	'Amazing Stories: Book Three' (Eric David Peterson)
1992	'City Of Joy' (Max Lowe)
1993	'Father Hood' (Jack Charles)
1995	'To Wong Foo, Thanks For Everything! Julie Newmar' (Vida Boheme)
1995	'Three Wishes' (Jack McCloud)
1998	'Black Dog' (Jack Crews)
1998	'Letters From A Killer' (Race Darnell)
2000	'Forever Lulu' (Ben Clifton)
2001	'Green Dragon' (Jim Lance)
2001	'Donnie Darko' (Jim Cunningham)
2002	'Waking Up In Reno' (Roy Kirkendall)
2003	'One Last Dance' (Travis MacPhearson)
2003	'11 : 14' (Frank)
2004	'Dirty Dancing : Havana Nights' (Dance Class Instructor)
2004	'George and the Dragon' (Garth)
2005	'Icon' (Jason Monk)
2005	'Keeping Mum' (Lance)
2006	'Fox and the Hound II' (Cash)
2007	'Jump!' (Richard Pressburger)

JENNIFER GREY

Jennifer Grey was already familiar with her co-star, Patrick Swayze, when she landed the role of Baby in 'Dirty Dancing'. The pair had acted together three years earlier in the film 'Red Dawn'.

Like Swayze, Jennifer came from a performing arts family – only hers was much more mainstream show-biz. Her grandfather is the American comedian and musician, Mickey Katz. Her father is the famous stage and screen actor, Joel Grey, who won an Oscar for his portrayal of the creepy nightclub host in 'Cabaret', and her mother is the singer, Jo Wilder.

The young Ms Grey's first public performance was a dance routine in an advert for Dr Pepper (everyone has to start somewhere!). This was followed by an appearance in an off-Broadway play called 'Album'. Her first TV appearance was in a PBS production, 'Media Probes', and she reached the big screen for the first time in the film 'Reckless'.

Following small roles in the films 'The Cotton Club' and 'American Flyers', Jennifer Grey really came to the public's attention playing the angry sister, Jeanie, in the 1986 cult hit 'Ferris Bueller's Day Off'. But it was 'Dirty Dancing' that made her into a worldwide star. To meet and fall in love with a handsome dance instructor older than yourself is a teenage girl's dream and Jennifer Grey as Baby is the focus of a universal female fantasy.

After the phenomenal success of 'Dirty Dancing', Jennifer Grey took a break from the limelight for several years. She returned in 1999 in a short-lived American sitcom called 'It's Like, You Know . . .' in which she played a struggling actress called . . . Jennifer Grey! (The performance also revealed some much-publicised plastic surgery on her nose.) She also appeared in an episode of 'Friends' and had a small part in the film 'Bounce' with Ben Affleck and Gwyneth Paltrow.

Jennifer was born on March 26, 1960 in New York and attended The Dalton School, an elite private school in the city. In 2001, she married the actor Clark Gregg and the couple have one daughter called Stella who was born on December 3, 2001.

JERRY ORBACH

Jerry Orbach was already a well-known and accomplished star of stage, film and television when he took the part of Baby's stern but kind-hearted father, Dr Houseman, in 'Dirty Dancing'.

He was born Jerome Bernard Orbach in the Bronx, New York City, on October 20, 1935. His father, Leon Orbach, was a German Jew and his mother, Emily Olexy, was a Polish-American Roman Catholic. He was brought up a Catholic, but his father's Jewish nature was always much in evidence on the screen.

The young Orbach had a disrupted childhood as his family moved Up-State and then on to Pennsylvania, Massachusetts and Illinois.

As a young man, he studied drama at the University of Illinois and then back in New York City at The Actors Studio.

He began his professional career on the Broadway and off-Broadway stage. He played the part of El Gallo in 'The Fantasticks', a show that ran for decades. He was nominated for a Tony Award for his performance in two great musicals, 'Guys and Dolls' and 'Chicago'. He received a Tony Award for Best Actor in a Musical for his part in 'Promises, Promises'.

His film career began way back in 1958 when he made his first big screen appearance in 'Cop Hater'. He had appeared in a further 12 films including 'The Sentinel' (1977) and 'Brewster's Millions' (1985) before he came to 'Dirty Dancing'. The instant success of the film further boosted his career and he went on to play a cold-blooded killer in Woody Allen's film, 'Crimes and Misdemeanors'. Then he worked for Disney as a voice-over artist in 'Beauty and the Beast' and 'Aladdin and the King of Thieves'.

It was on television that Jerry Orbach achieved his greatest amount of success. For no less than twelve years, from 1992-2004, he played the wisecracking detective, Lennie Briscoe, in the crime series 'Law and Order'. He was signed up to appear in the follow-up series, 'Law and Order: Trial by Jury', but his untimely death at the age of 69 meant he only appeared in the first two episodes. A subsequent episode was dedicated to his memory.

Orbach married his first wife, Marta Curro, in 1958. They had two sons, Anthony Nicholas and Christopher Ben. The couple divorced in 1975 and, in 1979, Jerry married Elaine Cancilla, a dancer whom he met in the musical, 'Chicago'.

Always at home in his native New York, he lived in a high-rise flat off Eighth Avenue. He was such a well-known and much-loved character in the local shops and restaurants that his friends have asked the City council to name a street after him.

When he died of prostate cancer on December 28, 2004, the whole of Broadway paid tribute to him by dimming the lights – one of the greatest honours in the American theatre.

Generous to the last, Orbach willed that his eyes should be used for transplants and now, thanks to him, two blind people are able to see.

JERRY ORBACH

Filmography

(Complete Career)

1958	'Cop Hater'
1961	'Mad Dog Call'
1964	'Ensign Pulver'
1965	'John Goldfarb, Please Come Home'
1971	'The Gang That Couldn't Shoot Straight'
1972	'A Fan's Notes'
1975	'Fore Play'
1977	'The Sentinel'
1981	'Underground Aces'
	'Prince of the City'
1985	'Brewster's Millions'
1986	'The Imagemaker'
	'F/X'
1987	'Dirty Dancing'
	'Someone To Watch Over Me'
1988	'I Love N.Y.'
1989	'Last Exit To Brooklyn'
1989	'Crimes and Misdemeanors'
1991	'Dead Women in Lingerie'
	'California Casanova'
	'Out for Justice'
	'Toy Soldiers'
	'Delusion'
	'Delirious'
	'Beauty and the Beast' (voiceover)
1992	'A Gnome Named Gnorm'
	'Straight Talk'

1992	'Universal Soldier'
	'Mr. Saturday Night'
1993	'The Cemetery Club'
1996	'Aladdin and the King of Thieves' (voiceover)
1999	'Temps'
2000	'The Acting Class' (cameo role)
2002	'Manna from Heaven'
2003	'Mickey's PhilharMagic' (voiceover)

CYNTHIA RHODES

Cynthia Rhodes came to her role as Penny with the highlights of her movie career already behind her. She shot to fame in 1983 in 'Flashdance', a film like 'Dirty Dancing' that is still shown today.

Born on November 21, 1956, in Nashville, Tennessee, Cynthia began her performing career as a singer and dancer. She made her professional debut on the stage of 'Opryland, USA' and stayed with the company for five years before moving on to television and appearing in the series 'Music Hall America'.

When she moved to Los Angeles, she was spotted by Kenny Ortega (later the choreographer for 'Dirty Dancing') who used her as a dancer in 'Xanadu' alongside Gene Kelly and Olivia Newton-John.

At the same time, she appeared in music videos for the pop group, Toto, and also worked as a dancer for the band, The Tubes, when they toured the States in the early Eighties.

1983 was Cynthia's year. As well as her smash-hit 'Flashdance', she appeared in the other big musical movie, 'Staying Alive'.

A role in 'Runaway' followed in 1984 – and then came 'Dirty Dancing'.

She disappeared from the big screen after that, returning to her roots as a singer and dancer.

At the end of the Eighties, Cynthia Rhodes was the singer for the pop group, Animotion. They had a top ten hit in America with a song called 'Room to Move'.

In 1989, Cynthia married singer-songwriter, Richard Marx. They have three sons called Brandon, Lucas and Jesse.

PART 4
DIRTY DANCING TRIVIA

Since its release on August 21, 1987, 'Dirty Dancing' has become a true cinema phenomenon. Hugely successful on so many fronts, the film has taken on a life of its own which, twenty years on, can now be detailed in full. So stand by for a plethora of fascinating facts about *the* dance movie from *the* decade of dance movies . . .

∗ 'Dirty Dancing' only cost approximately 3 million US dollars to make.

∗ To date, the film has generated over 170 million US dollars in box-office receipts alone, making it one of the biggest independent films of all time.

∗ So far, over 10 million Dirty Dancing DVDs have been sold and sales now average one million copies a year.

∗ The result of a recent survey, revealed a staggering 99% awareness among adults aged 18-54.

∗ In the story, Kellerman's Holiday Camp is supposedly located in the Catskill Mountains north of New York. In fact, the locations used for shooting the film were at Mountain Lake in Virginia and at Lake Lure in North Carolina.

∗ The film's writer, Eleanor Bergstein, based her screenplay on her memories of visiting similar holiday camps in the Catskills with her parents when she was a teenager.

* The film was set in the summer, yet the lake scene where they were practising the lift, was filmed in October. Since the leaves were already turning colour, they had to paint the background; if you look closely, you can see where they missed a few in one spot.

* The lake practice scene was filmed at Lake Lure in the mountains of North Carolina. There are no close-ups, because the actors were so cold, their lips were blue.

* Bergstein had to push hard for her script of 'Dirty Dancing' to be accepted by a film studio. She used to send it round with tapes of the songs that she imagined would accompany the action. Often, she found that the tapes were much more popular with the studio executives than the script!

* Val Kilmer was originally offered the lead male role, but declined.

* The soundtrack – including the Oscar-winning '(I've Had) The Time of My Life' has sold more than 41 million copies, making it one of the bestselling soundtracks of all time.

* The songs 'She's Like The Wind', co-written by Patrick Swayze and Stacy Widelitz and sung by Patrick Swayze, and Eric Carmen's 'Hungry Eyes', were both hit singles from the film.

* Despite their riveting on-screen chemistry, it is rumoured that Patrick Swayze and Jennifer Grey did not always get on during filming.

* The very famous scene, where Johnny and Baby are practising their dancing, and crawling towards each other on the floor, was actually just a warm-up for the real scene, and they were goofing around. The director liked it so much, he kept it in the film.

* In the scene where Johnny and Baby are practising the dancing and she keeps laughing when he runs his arm down hers, it was not part of the scene . . . she was actually laughing and his frustration was genuine. They left it in because it was effective. Her falling over in this scene, was also unplanned.

* Jennifer Grey, at 27, was 10 years older than the character of Baby. During her audition, she had five minutes to prove she could play younger, and that she had the moves for the role.

* Bruce Morrow ("Cousin Brucie"), the famous WABC announcer, provides the closing commentary for the movie and also plays a cameo role as the magician.

* 'Dirty Dancing' has a vast legion of female fans who regard the film as the ultimate romance. As a result of being such a powerful fantasy, it has sometimes been called 'the Star Wars for girls'.

* Patrick Swayze's name has spawned a number of popular phrases – 'Crazy like Patrick Swayze', 'Crazy over Swayze' and 'I'm Swayze'. (The latter means "I'm gone" – a reference to the actor's later role in 'Ghost'.)

* The curtain went up on the stage version of 'Dirty Dancing' in London's West End in October 2006. Producers say its £11 million advance sales, make the musical the fastest-selling show in West End stage history.

* Voted Number 2 'Must See Movie' of all time, by listeners of *Capital FM* in London.

Patrick Swayze, summed it up perfectly in a recent interview when he said . . .

"This is the movie that will not die."

CREDITS

'Dirty Dancing'

Starring Patrick Swayze, Jennifer Grey,
Cynthia Rhodes and Jerry Orbach
Written by Eleanor Bergstein
Directed by Emile Ardolino
Choreography by Kenny Ortega
Music score by John Morris
Music Consultant: Jimmy Lenner
Director of Photography: Jeff Jur
Produced by Linda Gottlieb
Co-Producer: Eleanor Bergstein
Associate Producer: Doro Bachrach
Executive Producers: Mitchell Cannold and
Steven Reuther
Edited by Peter C. Frank

A Linda Gottlieb Production

© Lions Gate Entertainment Inc.

219

The End

The End